Maps of Injury

Sundress Publications • Knoxville, TN

ISBN: 978-1-951979-01-0
Library of Congress: 2020930344
Published by Sundress Publications
www.sundresspublications.com

Editor: Jeremy Michael Reed
Editorial Assistants: Anna Black and Erin Elizabeth Smith
Editorial Interns: Quinn Carver, Erica Hoffmeister, Kimberly Ann Priest, Jacquelyn Scott, and Ada Wofford

Colophon: This book is set in Adobe Garamond Pro.

Cover Art: "Minar River" by Nelson Minar

Cover Design: Kristen Ton

Book Design: Erin Elizabeth Smith

Maps of Injury
Chera Hammons

Acknowledgments

I would like to express my appreciation to the editors of the following publications, in which some of the poems in this manuscript first appeared:

Amarillo-Globe News: "Bounding Flight" (reprint)
The Apogee: "Phlebotomy" (winner of the Emily Stauffer Poetry Prize)
Arcturus: "The Onion as a Vessel of Memory"
Blue Fifth Review: "Hook Echo"
Cider Press Review: "Evergreen"
Common Good Books: "Bounding Flight"
drafthorse: "Calling In"
Foundry: "Limit"
The Fourth River: "What Happens Then"
The Maine Review: "Bible Belt"
Qu: "Accelerate"
Rattle: "Shriven"
Rattle: Poets Respond: "Descent of the Germanwings"
Ruminate: "Black Horse I am Breaking"
Rust + Moth: "The Capacity for Malignancy is Ancient" and "Pathologies"
Stoneboat: "Autocorrect"
Up the Staircase Quarterly: "Poem for the Body Found Nearby"
Valparaiso Poetry Review: "Bridling"

Table of Contents

Eye, Ear, Throat, Mouth

Heart; Stomach

Epilogue

To you, readers: to your invisible struggles and triumphs, whatever they may be, and all you've overcome.

and

To Daniel, who has learned to appreciate poetry and has carried infinite boxes of books for me.

Amnesties

I am trying again to learn how to live
with you, body. This skin is such a map of injury now.

So softly have you betrayed us
that the borders of discord bleed

into each other, smudged riverbanks and muddied water.
You granted quarter to enemies, let them sleep

in our rooms and eat from the cast iron pans
we have spent our whole generation seasoning.

How the warhorses mill about
over biopsied fields where the battles wore scars,

and no trees will ever grow there again.
That first misunderstanding, body—

can you remember where it started:
belly button. Birthmark.

If I lose sight of you moving through the darkness
this time, forgive me.

Monuments must not be built for us, body.
What we must learn here is not our loneliness.

Skin and Limb

Cross-section of an Oak

This year was a thin year. See how closely this ring follows
the one before. Too much heat, maybe. Not enough rain.
The ground cracked and the leaves curled like questions.
The animals, too, must have suffered then.
If you follow these lines back with your finger,
you'll see that it wasn't the first disaster.
There are other landmarks here, scars
that must have been from lightning or parasites;
here's a blemish that started years ago
and made the tree grow unevenly most of its life.
Before that, see—black stain where it survived a fire.
The past is always told with lines, layers of sediment
where the fossils are found, cores of icebergs
that show what was and what is disappearing,
the creases of skin around the eyes and mouth.
Even our toenails, in times of disease or malnourishment,
develop ridges that separate normalcy from catastrophe.
An uncovered foot can tell all your secrets:
Last month, I never went hungry. The month before, I was poor.
Under bark mottled and silent as the deer,
the tree is always mapping its history.
One year, the early spring snowmelt woke its roots,
and it stretched itself into plenty.
Another, the tree could not bring itself
to get that much farther from its heart.

Evergreen

What we fear may not come to pass. Though the wind this year has been violent,
and the sky rainless, the tree we planted in front of our house

because we imagined some kind of life there, some green hope,
some shelter from the weather and the neighbors, may survive.

As I drive to work, my car filters in the woody smell of smoke
from the grassfires beside the highway, and the sunrise is as red as it will be at the end.

In a spring like this, the topsoil blows away, and the ground is hard, unforgiving.
Just yesterday, my black colt came up lame, short-stepping and dragging a hind toe.

He knew only I could help him, but there was no blood, heat, or swelling tissue—
nothing to show me what hurt. A strained muscle, maybe. A stone bruise.

Today in Brussels, the planes are grounded, bright birds sunning on the tarmac
while the edges of glass shimmer beneath. This morning, people like us,

holding whatever they thought to take with them,
ran down the dark tracks in shadowed tunnels toward uncertain ideas of air and light

while smoke billowed behind them, quiet as the voice of a ghost.
None of them knew soon enough that they wouldn't make it to work this time,

that they would be given new reasons to run, that what had already happened
would become more frightening than the darkness that lay ahead.

We are lucky. This afternoon, I'll check the horse's leg again (he is gentle, and won't kick), feel down the thin tendons that keep him on his feet, see if anything has changed.

I'll haul water to the tree, prick myself with its needles, kneel to feel the ground around it. I'll worry, as I so often have, that I can't do enough to make it live.

Fall Equinox

Early morning, it's dark enough now
to draw the rabbits out.
When my headlights catch two young cottontails,
they freeze, white with spectral eyes,
and I must either brake or hit them.
Farther down, at the stop sign,
a jackrabbit lopes before me
with the awkward grace of a yearling colt,
all length and joints and hunger,
and I watch it disappear into the brush.

People hit rabbits on this road all the time.
Those I left alive in the morning
are often laid out on the shoulder when I come home.

Sometimes, from over their bodies, hawks take off.
Sometimes, they will lie there rotting for days.

It's times like this I wonder if I will make it.
Not because I drive so often
when I am only half awake,
and for so far;
not because I compare my mortality
to the rabbit's.

But because someone behind me
couldn't stop, or didn't.
Because I never know if I can.

Calling In

I won't say where I am going.

The tally of crows gets higher. They rise
from telephone poles and fence posts.

They look like scraps of black garbage bags
loosened from branches.

I won't say where I am going, but today,
there are no rooms of dissatisfied children

who are hungry, or a beige office
that has carpet pressed as close to the ground

as it can get, and walls that are cold,
and no windows with light that reaches in.

The phone will cry and cry all the time.
I am not going, as I told them,

to have my temperature taken by quiet people in white coats
whose stairwell smoke sticks like a fog to their shoulders.

I don't have to talk about the weather.

I don't have to tell anyone, if they ask, that I am going
neither to heaven nor to hell,

with no belief in either. I might say this:
that the trees stretch from the earth in the medians,

raising their arms to the sun
and growing heavier the farther they get from ground,

but even the ones beside the road
are beautiful in their leaning,

each one a different shape against its own allotment of wind.
Out of the treeline, a lone coyote hesitates,

then steps, shimmering in the lifting heat,
onto the shoulder of the highway.

Why I Will Choose Cremation

For a long time, aside from how she lay, she looked alive,
fur brushy and red, tail with its black tip.

It was all I could do not to pull over and test
the softness of a fox's coat.

Every hair rippled in wake of the cars
as it must have before in an autumn wind,
shifting the browns and golds, making the shades quiver.

In junior high science, we saw a video about decomposition.

A fox had died under a tree, and in time-lapse
we saw the fox turn white under squirming maggots,

distend, then shrink, and finally disappear,
leaving only bits of copper skin, a jaw, the tail.

We watched first its eyes, then its tongue fall to pieces.

It was messy, but no one looked away.

This time, it wasn't like that. I drove by the fox's body
every day, and she shrank; cleanly and simply,

but still, there was less of her every time I looked.

Now she seems just an emptied version of herself.

Thousands of people drive by her as they leave the city,
and her skull, like an omen, swallows them.

I know I will watch for her long after she is gone,
think of the black tips, the fur with its depths,
the body that once stalked rabbits by the highway.

Already, without noticing, I have stopped wanting to stop.

Broke

As the water rises, the horses lighten. Rain thrums
like static in the stillness. They spill over

into the creek. They become nothing but themselves.
The sweat lines wash out from behind their elbows and ears.

Except for their shoes, they may as well be wild—
even the bay, which someone trained to lead when it was days old

by releasing a hold once it had stepped forward,
when it learned to give in until it would follow anyone.

Now it swims against the current, legs pointed and tipping,
toward the others, who have gathered in the last corner.

The hidden fence between them, like a shipwreck, snags it,
and it struggles, tendons thrusting through wire, in silence.

From the road, onlookers speak as it drowns about
how they can help without getting kicked,

wrapped in a rope, knocked out, or pulled under.
All they are able to do yet is talk.

How strange it is that someone valued these horses enough
to fence them in, then left them when the flood came.

Let us not so easily turn away from what we have bound.
This is how, for a moment, it is possible to think

that the first person you married did not intend,
in the beginning, to break your heart.

Because no one else can stand to watch the horses die,
men and women are jumping into the water now to save them.

They believe us enough to follow us out;
horses are trained to ignore the most exquisite betrayals.

One by one, they are guided to the bank. See how carefully
they step up, scattering drops that look like jewels.

Phlebotomy

Tell me again how I share with the deer
more than a kinship to curled spring leaves,
shadow-dapples, wild tendernesses.
I'm still not sure I know how to listen
now that I miss turns, misspell words.
I know my body, like theirs,
would rearrange itself for a bullet.
No wonder it accommodates so easily
a needle whose language finds its tongue
in eight vials of blood that comes out slowly.
That's what we're all made of, untidy warmth
thick with uncertainty and dark,
with legs like wine when the nurse tilts it
to put on the label that has a name.
Imagine the tick as small as a poppy seed
burrowing into the soft crease of the knee,
years of holding its disease after it has fallen away.
To have a child is to know it will suffer.
The box rattles with samples of us.
Our blood travels like prayer
to its houses of answers.

Bone

The Capacity for Malignancy is Ancient

The woman on the gallery floor says yes when I ask
if I can photograph the fossil of *Protorohippus venticolum*
that has the plaque naming it "The Dawn of Horses."

It's actually the only replica we have in the store, she says,
and shows me photographs of the original,
which has the same black horse shape,
black splintered ribs, nestled among prehistoric fish
in the sandy rock. His tail is missing, she says,
but it might just be under the fish.

How the ancestor of horses ended up on a lake bottom
is a mystery as complex as ours.
On Facebook, my friend posts the announcement

that at least one type of cancer existed in humans
nearly two million years ago,
that the bone of a foot has been discovered
with the same cells as those that make us sick.

This way, we can confirm that death doesn't need to evolve.

I still remember the spiral of tissue from the breast biopsy
floating in the fluid in the little jar, how I couldn't lift
a gallon of milk or I'd start to bleed.

I am wearing the necklace that belonged
to my maternal grandmother, who died
and took her cancer with her when she was 24.

We wear fragile bodies, and now it would seem
that they have always known how to turn against us,
though there are so many other kinds of endings we could find.

No matter where we go, we walk on bones.

The gallery is air conditioned and clinical,
and its most stunning fossil is the only one that's a replica,
a horse that is dog-sized and has toes instead of hooves.

The way it lies on its side reminds me
of the horse I had to euthanize because of tumors.

The man with a backhoe dug a ramp into a grave.
I led the horse to the bottom and the vet let him down
in stages. We watched him die to make sure
he wouldn't know that he was being buried.

There used to be a mound over him, but now there is nothing.

I left his halter on so that whoever finds him
will understand that he was loved.

Hard Water

We draw poor water; it coats
the glasses, the appliances, our skin
with white ovals of mineral
and turns us all to salt from the inside out,
but it does keep us alive in a dry country
when nothing else could.

Here, where the sky could never give us enough,
we would wait forever for the rain,
watching our horses shrink into models of bones
while the dust walks over the land in brown columns.
This is our history. We started with nothing.
Then our ancestors learned how to dig.

Some of the old windmills still turn
though blades are missing,
and the rudders hang and creak.
Livestock are born knowing how to wait
while the water pumps from the thin pipe.
From the cool algae bottoms of the tanks, bullfrogs
send up orbs of stolen air.

Neighbors ask each other, *How deep is your well?*
Three hundred feet to the Ogallala.
Five hundred to the Santa Rosa.
We find the nearest lakes that were buried alive.

How long the water has waited there in its cool room,
gathering calcium to stain our surfaces,
until our house is as full of minerals
as the earth under our feet.

This water turns us into old men and widows
and never replenishes itself.

It is hard. It is hard. It never gets any easier.
Why do we live here? we ask each other,
where the land is flat and tough and everything is against us,

and the answer, so simple
we can't allow ourselves to consider it:
someone who came before us drilled a well.

Poem for the Body Found Nearby

I.

Maybe you were a bad one.
Maybe you had this one coming.

Maybe you were only alone,
and that's why no one missed you.

Maybe there is a report to acknowledge your loss,
but the math of the missing hasn't been done yet.

Today we are only guessing how much you gave
to those tall weeds, too far off the road for the county to mow.

They say that it will take months to find out.
Until then, our sympathy belongs to the dead.

And to ourselves, who deserve to know that we are passing ghosts
as we flaunt our brilliant and worrisome lives.

II.

We want to know you mattered.

So many people think you might belong to them
that they arrive one by one, though no one asked them to come.

A mother goes under the yellow tape to see
if there is anything she recognizes:
a button, a ring, a shoe. The spine of a wallet.

Our sympathy goes to the living.

Men in uniform comb the ground with their gloves.

They look for your name and other imprints
of the body we made transparent for over a year.

You only tell us what we already know:

Someone will always teach us what loss is like.
Someone will always teach us how to grieve.

III.

Some light is wrong for taking pictures in.
A good photographer might say not to frame the sunset.

Turn instead to catch the shadows— that's where the interest lies,
the tall dark pillars that slant away from it

and cleave the landscape to the deepening horizon.
In this disarming flatness, this expanse of wind,

every building from miles away slants back,
every metal tower leans, the colt stands

on its unclosed knees and reaches the edge of darkness,
and the hawks that shift and tremble in the thermals

melt over the silencing earth.
Even the buzzards here don't speak to anyone.

You, too, know what it is like to wander in emptiness
looking for artifacts. Whose last words

haven't eventually become *I loved someone*?
A body can hide in this ochre plain,

soft and still, for months while its stories unravel.
They are gathering now the skull, the shoes,

locking hands to comb the ditches.
The only news we hear is that there is nothing new.

The mirror behind the lens lifts so briefly
to let the light through.

If someone asks you, *Am I a good person*?
say *Yes*. No one will ask it twice.

We fumble in the dusk, where it is hard to see each other.
This is the kind of light in which we must hurry.

Our sight comes in flashes and blurs,
shapes that seem familiar.

Beside that quiet congregation of trees,
someone starts to catalog the bones.

Bison for Sale

These are poor representatives of wilderness,
rough beasts in wire fences with yellow straw bales
fallen open and churned into ground around them.

Beside the highway and muddy to their knees,
they who could once swim the widest rivers
grow insensitive to the tractor-trailers rushing past
and lower their horns as they sleep on hard hooves.

They have learned to live wherever they are placed
with much more grace than I have,
and when I drive by the sign advertising them
I think about how it would be to bring two back with me
to put into my snakeweed and yucca pasture.

It is not much, but wide and bright, at least.
I would buy them, if only to watch them
walk my few acres and look off into the canyon behind us
and dream. Here there are deer and foxes to be scented,
a wind that sings almost constantly. The privilege
of imagining there is plenty.

When I feel my home is not where I belong,
that there is nothing left here for me, that my body
is a stranger with whom I must compromise,
I have only to look to the horizon, the many careful stitches
holding sky to land, for a moment of kind forgetfulness.

I can't afford to offer this to them or to anyone;
I don't really have it to give. But if it is true
that we contain some of the memories of our grandparents,
perhaps bison are already made
of souls that understand how to be unbound,
and when they stand and dream,
it is of wandering.

For them, too, sunlight and space must surely drive back
these other, darker vistas. Generations of birth and death in fences.
The years of almost-disappearance. The starvation
of those old, free winters. The white hunters who,
in fading photographs, stood on stacks of skulls.

imagining horses on the quail canyon trail

the last night of summer   the canyon called us out
already starting   to fill   with darkness
lower down   where the wind couldn't reach
the sunflowers drooped their heavy hearts   and waited
while quiet praying mantises fed on their mates   in the dark
we stopped   at the boundary tree   one of us tripped on
the pelvic bone of a deer unburied   after the rain
white and grained like   driftwood the sharpness smoothed off
(seaglass, smooth and cool)   you feared the horses   would stumble on it
next time we brought them down   and kicked it
into the dry creek bed to rattle and   be still   I mourned it.
we stood then and listened   to nothing for a while
soon we will float back like ghosts   on our transparent feet
toward the light we have left on
dishes piled in the kitchen   uneven attitude of chairs
even the television posturing to emptiness
to go inside again   always, like awakening the sudden sound and the light
you were so sure
I didn't feel like telling you   horses are not the same as we are
they do everything they can to keep
        from lingering over bones

Pathologies

According to the internet, I have all the symptoms
of leukemia. When I tell my husband this,
he is appropriately concerned. He reads over my shoulder,
Bone pain. Fever. Fatigue. Weakness.

I feel worse just watching him read it,
so I stand and go to the window
where the cat sits watching yellow and orange wasps
buzzing against invisibility
and behind that, a field of horses too young to ride,
their wolf teeth intact, their knees not yet closed.

At odd times, I remember how the doctors
thought I had brain cancer when I was thirteen.
All the scans they did.

My thumbprint is on the glass at eye level
where I tried to smash one of the gnats
that make their way into our house every spring.
It swirls perfectly now over a hazy smear of clouds.

Should you go to the doctor? my husband asks,
but I have already told him about how my doctor
listens to my symptoms with his head to one side, like a robin's,
then prescribes anti-depressants, no matter what I have told him
about where it hurts.

Get a new doctor, he says. It sounds easy
when someone puts it like that.

Outside the window, a spider is walking,
twitching its many green eyes.
When I move my finger underneath it, it jumps.

A reflexologist once told me
that you carry all of your mother's grief
in the arch of your foot.
I took off my shoes and lay back.
I worried about whether my feet were nice enough
for him to want to touch.

He could tell me in such technical terms the reasons
for the urge to sob when he pressed my sole
with his thumb— the connection between the infant
and the walls of its mother,
the shared cells transferring everything.

All I really wanted to know, what I couldn't ask,
was how such sadness could bear so much weight.

Accelerate

The half-light before sunrise flattens the field,
doesn't leave shadows yet, draws the road
with graphite stillness, the flat mesquites
that spike against the toneless sky, fences
as monochromatic as the memory of pain.

Watching for mule deer is the main thing,
because they are as gray as the hill
at times like these, will leap in front of you
with wild desperation, some mislaid instinct,
their eyes a flash in the headlights
before the quick blur of sharp hooves and
splintering bones as thin as a bird's.

The dented front will tell it, the stiff short hairs
hanging off the curve of the bumper.
The suffering thing you don't know what to do with.
The way you'll walk back, hoping no one will know it was you.

I've heard that, if you know you're going to hit one,
you should accelerate right before you do,
so that the car will hunker like a cat
and glance it up across the hood, increasing your chance
of survival, if not the deer's.

It must be this light—it's the light that does it to us.
Bright enough to show the form of the world
without giving any definition to it.
The way the early morning makes no promises,
might as well tell that nothing at all is there:
not the car's headlights fading into the gray light,
or the road that looks like it closes behind you.
Not the invisible city that soon the sun will rise over.
Not the brokenness you leave behind
that carries your name.

Ribs

Everything here
rattles with emptiness.

Milkweed pods.
Devil's claws. Feed bins.
Water barrels.

The prairie, an empty basin.

The dogs have made hollows
in the shapes of their bodies
and lie cradled in the hot dust.

The yearling colts, become taller
than their appetites can keep up,
are all open knees and spine.

They too are empty,
not yet being in work.
They graze in long, slow shadows.

The wind turbines stand with still blades
in the wavering heat.

The dogs
whine in their sleep. This

is August. This

is a bone month. The leaves curl
in, drawing nearer their veins.

This day is as meant for living
as every other day has been.

Eye, Ear,
Throat, Mouth

After Another, I Don't Think

Not thinking, I have left the television on again
and gone out to the flowers while it tallies the dead
to an empty room.

The silence in the beds is broken only
by the clip of my shears deadheading roses.
The hips are just thickening, turning to fruit,

the faces of them like many-pointed stars.
I don't ask why I need the roses to try longer for beauty.
I simply cut, and they allow it.

But the roses are not supposed to mean anything here.
A young rabbit crouches in the shade, watching me work.
I don't think I want it to learn to fear me, though it will.

How people talk. It is enough to know that no one will save us.
Not thinking, I have finished tidying the roses. The rabbit
has slipped away. The ground is littered with bruised pink petals.

The blank stems with their blunt green ends stare.
I used to be with a man who was an alcoholic.
He never understood, the next clear day,

the damage he had done while he was drunk.
He wanted to believe whatever story in which he lost the least.
Each time, it was the same. The blame, the back-and-forth.

We were hostages. Finally I gave up on arguing with him,
would just watch him open the next bottle and start counting.
Even if he moved too abruptly toward me

when he was still sober, I'd flinch.
What are you so afraid of? he'd ask, though he must have known.
Nothing, I would tell him, thinking, *This.*

Fire Weather

Don't tell me you've never thought of just sitting back
and watching it all go up in flames. You might as well,

when there's so little that can be done.
Every windy day, the land around us burns,

and we watch the smoke rise, afraid that this time,
our home will fall, too. The walls we lifted turned to cinders.

The exquisite horses become black bone.
So far today, four fatalities, all people who tried to save

cattle that were likely going to end up at slaughter.
When I see smoke, it is all tied up now with death and livelihoods.

Maybe love, too. The relentless, wordless consumption of it.
The sacrifices. The wildlife refuge posts a video of deer leaping

desperately before the heat, and you can't help but mourn for them.
Now my Facebook feed is all politics, fear, memes, and hunger interspersed

with photographs of jagged orange lines, gray plumes
that go up for miles, and tire-tracked black and smoldering ground.

Calls for prayer. Stories of animals burning in their barns.
Lamentations of this drought, how our lips split and bleed in the wind,

the feel of clay dust in our teeth, the acrid air. Our spring is a short,
cruel season of birth and casualty. If someone leaves

without saying goodbye here, it is only because they left too early
to do it. Eventually we will hear that the fires have been contained,

but you can't trust them; they smoke and reignite days later,
sometimes, the same way the headless body of the rattlesnake

strikes where it last remembers your shadow standing.
Everything here holds so hard onto whatever it can.

As much as we know we shouldn't, that it's not worth it,
we run into fire to save what is still alive and ours.

When we turn on the evening news, the weather map fills
with approaching green. It's too dark for us to see outside.
For a second, we hope. For a while, we'll be safe again.

Then the meteorologists tell us how their radars
interpret the smoke as rain.

Youth Group

The day I forgot to memorize my verses,
I memorized instead the inside of the restroom stall

at the community center where our doomsday cult met.
It was my punishment for forgetting:

to stand in that stuffy corner with the cold tiles, those blank blue walls.
That loneliness. I studied how the sides bolted together,

trying to remember the book's name and which words came first.
I drew pictures in my head. I imagined horses.

I thought of questions I wanted to ask,
like *Where do the pheasants nest?*

I could have crawled out under the partition
or unlocked the door, but I didn't.

No one could tell me in a way I'd understand
why the weekly recitations mattered.

I had discovered they were on no report card.
I thought I already knew all of the secrets in the Bible,

could tell anyone who asked the most important lesson—
that if you see an angel, there will soon be some kind of test.

I already suspected that everyone but me
had been called by a name that meant something.

Chair Test

In the room, there was a cassette recorder,
a music stand, and silence,

the cocoon of wood paneling too warm,
enough to make you play sharp.

How young we were then,
when the most important distinction

was first clarinet. I used to think
the practicing mattered,

would memorize my music at home
because my eyes were weak

and I couldn't read it in the school's
flickering fluorescent lighting.

I didn't want anyone to know
I worked twice as hard for talent.

Now that I know better,
I imagine the band director

and his assistants ignoring the tapes
we made in that close room,

discussing instead who they thought
would be most likely to choke on stage

when it came to the solo.

But that never occurred to me then.

All it came down to was that room,
the cassette recorder, the silence

I thought I could defeat.

Those simple instructions:

Press record. State your name.
Hope that the song you bring with you

is as good as how you practiced it.

Believe we won't be guessing,
that our guesses are never wrong.

Where We Meet

Since I found out I'm allergic to dogs,
I dream of them trotting towards me out of a twilight,
tongues hanging soft and wet as clean sheets.

Their faces blur and refocus like those of the children
I will never have.
They run more quickly as they get closer,

and I wait for my throat to close off my breath.
Even in my dream, it always happens.
But the dogs themselves are friendly, not frightening;

their tails hit my calves as they circle me.
They don't know why I back away.
They grin. The worst are the injured ones

that appear from nowhere to beg me for some kind
of mercy, how I can't make them understand
how little I am able to help even myself.

In the waking world, I still find my hand
reaching to touch dogs when I see them on sidewalks,
in cool green parks, then I remember and draw back.

How quietly they have moved from the everyday,
the things I don't think much about,
to the same world in which I wander hallways

looking for a classroom I haven't seen since high school,
where tree roots buckle the speckled floor
and a coyote drags off the carcass of a deer.

Everyone from my past waits in that place,
former coworkers, forgotten friends, my old loves,
and now the dogs.

The dogs alone, I never thought to see there.
It is as if my body has rejected their kind of faith.
And all of those ghosts just try to keep from disappearing.

I try to forget them, though it is my fault we are divided.
At night, the dogs are as glad to be near me
as they ever have been. They have sought me even

in darkness. Here, in this passage of half-familiar doors,
where we, too, would find an opening.

The Descent of the Germanwings

Musicians know how to write silence,
how to lay lines and measures across a white landscape,

to show where music is and where it can't be,
where notes should swell and where they should rest.

If I were a musician, I might write it this way:
empty measure after empty measure, then the cymbal left ringing out.

Everyone would know what I meant then.
But poetry doesn't speak with silence the way music can.

It can give you images: the slow drop through a tent of cloud.
The way the land stretches forever in veins of rock and snow.

It can put spaces in between things to spread them out.
The baby's cry hanging in the air, caught as in a photograph

with the same strange stillness as a horse caught mid-stride.
The metal glittering sharp as ice around the flanks of the Alps.

The fragments of bodies gathered and lifted out
of where they fell, as gently held as early asters,

or love letters smuggled through a war.
If I were a musician, I could write it another way, too:

I could unroll the lines of the staff like a fence.
The notes would settle all over it like wrens.

Then they would sing, if they felt a song there.

Bridling

The black colt was teething, so it seemed as good a time as any
to introduce him to the bit. He had already been mouthing
the rusted fence posts, the lip of the metal water trough,
the stalks of the yuccas, the toes of boots and hoods of jackets.
While the other horses were saddled and waiting,
he would chew on their stirrups, their reins.
The steel snaffle inlaid with its bright bars of copper
didn't seem like so much of a stretch anymore.
When the colt saw it offered, he took it without suspicion.
All that had to be done was to slip the headstall over his ears,
buckle it, and wait for him to get used to it.
He seemed confused by the persistence of it,
but not alarmed, just stood raising and lowering his head and chewing,
salivating foam and pieces of hay, thinking about it, with
the bit clanking dully as it bent to his tongue.
Everyone knew what that metallic sound foreshadowed
but him: the clank of shanks, curb chains, spurs. The breaking.
Once his mouth was quiet, his training done,
the bridle came off as easily as it went on,
with great care taken not to bump the young teeth.
He reached for the bit again as soon as it was out,
and we let our breath out with relief— that he had taken
the whole session so well, and that the copper inlay,
as it was meant to do, had already turned sweet in his mouth.

Bible Belt

This is the town that everyone drives through.
Those cows standing in the fog beside the road,

black coats beaded with morning mist,
and the donkeys watching over them, scarred

from battles with coyotes and feral dogs and frostbite:
we know them. They are ours.

We are the dry line, too, where the wind
teaches people to talk too loudly to each other.

Where the clouds gather into white cathedrals
 before they move east to rain—

we can't help but think they must have prayed harder than we did there.
I had another dream that my first husband tried to kill me.

With his hands, this time, and I could feel
that my throat was collapsing into silence

under the warmth and roughness of his palms.
I couldn't make a sound anyone would hear.

What is this dream trying to teach me to be afraid of?
I stayed, but he was only passing through.

Don't believe anyone here, except the mesquites, which never lie,
which send their leaves out only at the right time,

and build their poisoned thorns
wherever they have been injured.

We are a town where it could be worse.
Where you have to know someone.

Where spring shudders into summer
and summer drops like a handful of pennies into fall.

Where the highway, from a distance, flickers at night
as if it is a line of fireflies, not weary truck drivers

who flash their lights across the lanes to say
that the margin between them is narrow,

but that there is room, somewhere in that darkness,
to pass.

Hook Echo

To the east, tornadoes drop and then reenter cloud
as the black wall rolls back before the shining sunset,
trailing its jagged fringes of rain
so that it looks like one side of the earth is in shadow,
but where we stand is the middle of light and dark.
And the light that is left is bruised yellow-blue,
and the flag hangs though minutes before it had fought
as if it would tear from its cables and fly to another country.
The blue flax near the house, or the stems that are left,
closed its flowers early, pelted by stones of ice
that fell like cold stars, and believing it was already night.
The flowers won't have time to open again before night falls.
The way they nod, closed, at the remaining day,
as if acknowledging that they have given it up
and had no choice in it, today another in the list of
the things that don't hear goodbyes.
The last part of the day blazes, having borne away the weather.
The horses graze in the west on wet buffalo grass,
their heads down, dripping bodies outlined in light.

Googling *Borrelia burgdorferi*

It is natural to want to see what has destroyed me,
so I look up pictures on the internet.

It's a simple spiral under the microscope
next to blood cells that look like fat buttons.

It twists like a loose thread, worm
in the flesh of the green peach,
corkscrews into blood, organ, spinal fluid, brain.

How strange to see for myself the sickness
that took so long to name. Now it colors everything.

The mysterious hours of fever. The afternoons
hazy with fatigue. The gray spots drifting in the sea
of my sight. The days I got lost reading or counting

and couldn't find my way back. All the mornings
in high school when my fingers hurt too much to play
my clarinet, so I slipped where I could
into the sound of others, making me unreliable.

Now, everything makes sense.
It's no wonder I was never a soloist.

I count my heartbeats and learn what it is to wait.

I notice when there's a good day.

While my husband drives me to the grocery store,
my loudest conversations are with the passenger-side window:

the sighs of the antelope lying in the young green wheat.

The quick yellow melody of a meadowlark on a post.

The pale reflection of my own face flying silently over the fields
like either a ghost or a god.

Staked Plains

Even in this endless sea of grasses there are sirens
that call from the wrecks of their solitude.

You know their song. You have heard it, too.
It is high and fleeting, unsure as an animal.

Anyone who is from this place knows what I mean,
when relentless wind suddenly sounds so like a voice
that you look out to see if the neighbor's children
have come to play in your treeless yard.

But the dogs aren't barking; the horses' heads are down.
You are, it seems, the only one who hears it.

It's like the time you saw a bird die in flight,
when it fell into the road, and the cars just kept going
though the bird lay still, become unmade.

People were impatient for you to keep going.

This sadness. You unreel a bit more of yourself
each time you listen for it.

Though you haven't seen a coyote for days,
at night you think it is they who wake you,
their half-hysteria just on the other side of where you sleep.

The owls, too, seem to be always in the wind,
calling to each other of lost loves.

It begins to be beautiful, these bits of broken solitude.

The prairie makes room for you within her emptiness.

But be wary of it. If you too often hear the wind rattle the stalks,
when the rattlesnake sends its warning,
it will be to weight that is already shifting down.

And the filter that is your body— the chambers
separating blood with oxygen from blood without,
the lungs rising and falling like tides,
the membrane of your skin— is meant to allow pain.

With every breath, then, let the dangerous world in.

Listen without getting lost. Want to live.
Can you remember what age you were when you gave up
on your own music?

When you forgot that this land can turn into your loneliness?

That whatever song it is that draws you
becomes your song?

Standard Time

The days are so short now that we leave in darkness
and return in darkness. Against the barely blushing sky

the dying sunflowers hang, burdened by summer,
too heavy now to face the sun.

Someone has shorn the wheat and carried it off.
From the pasture between night and day, a lost cow lows

its loneliness. While the horses sleep, their coats grow long,
but every spring, the appaloosa sheds into a different atlas.

The spots always change. Black dog, whose face is turning white—
all night she barks, but at dawn, she is silent.

What is home? The years shift around it.
Doctors have learned to name our many illnesses.

The orb weavers have tied their children to the posts.
The sunflowers must bow to drop their seeds.

The deer watch from the shoulder of the road where
they quiet the instinct to run into the brightness.

Saying to each other, *be still. Wait.*
Saying *don't give up*.

Heart; Stomach

The Long Definition

The first lesson I learned as a young poet
was never to use the word *love*.
Teachers marked it with red *X*s
and told me that it has too many different meanings,
is too vague to evoke an image.
Show love instead, they'd suggest.

The older I got, the more I saw how right they were.
When I said *love*, my first husband heard *worship*.
I really meant, *I would give almost anything*.

Some people see love as a lost child waiting
for a warm bed, new clothes;
if the child runs away, they sit in the road and weep.

Some see it as a rare flower slowly blooming,
then fading. Some, a cancer that takes over.
Some, an enemy that should be made to surrender.

Some see Mount Everest, clean and imposing.
To reach the summit they must pass the bodies
of the ones who died trying,
and they fear that they will also become landmarks
that measure elevation.

Some see love as music, unfolded notes
on straight lines across a white page.

These are not all or not even close to all,
but you get the idea. *Love* can be
nothing or everything. What it means

is that we are willing to attempt something
outside of ourselves. Or that we are not.
You try explaining it.

While you do, two people, born strangers,
lie listening to each other breathe
in the quiet hours before dawn, able to believe,

for one more day, that words don't get lost
in the space between them. That an ancient tower
never fell and divided languages. That the only reason
we need such translation is to appease a jealous God.

Morning Chores

I check the horse trough for ice every winter morning.
My father used to be the one to do it, in the sharp dark dawn

before I left for school. While I had breakfast, he would step
into the cold with rubber boots and fleece-lined gloves, trailed by his breath.

Now I am the one to go through the cringing winter
on the moonblacked path that leads to the barn.

Sometimes when I arrive, there is a light glass sheet
that shimmers over the water. I barely press down to crack it.

The fault line spreads in bounds and hesitations
until the whole thing will shatter with one more touch.

The broken ice bobs on the surface, brittle and thin.

Sometimes, the ice is inches thick, and I heft a mallet and heave
my weight at it over and over, losing warmth in every swing.

The sound echoes off of the house, making a distant dog bark.
The horses come up from the pasture when they hear it,
looking for water, their manes and eyelashes frosted white.

If they have run from the far field, steam rises from them.

Later, I drive to work past the cows that lie against the fence
with frost on their black backs, past the tree that has one leaf
still hanging on, but the morning chore is still with me.

I wonder things, like: are they drinking from the place I made for them?
If I weren't there to do it, would they eat the snow instead,
let it melt against their graypink gums and trickle down
cold and wild, the way it fell?

I think about, too, how I sometimes find a crooked hole
nose-wide, where a horse has breathed its warmth out onto the ice
so long before my arrival that it has melted its own place to drink.

How the liquid beneath the ice then seems mysterious and dark,
as strange as a bruise I can't remember getting.

How it's just starting to glaze back over when I find it.
But that doesn't happen often. Usually, they wait for me to do it,
unworried and gentle in their faith that someone will appear

and give them water. Someone always has: lately,
the bundled woman who comes from a world not their own;

and long before, a man who didn't know he taught them
what to believe about love.

Apocalypse Coffee

My husband has found a recipe on the internet,
and we spend the afternoon picking faded gold mesquite beans

from the tree by the barn. For every good one,
there's one with a tiny hole, and we toss those

to the horses, who chew the sugar out
and don't care about the worms inside.

As we pick, we talk about how the soldiers
in other centuries learned to make this kind of coffee

between battles, when the regular kind had run out.
We agree it's good to know how to do something different, to adapt.

I wonder what I'll do if everything falls apart.
Or maybe it's not that the whole world ends,

but only our world ends, the two of us as we are now,
watching each other over something we made together

as the cream blooms and swirls up from its dark cup.
Ever since I found out I was sick, I can't stop thinking

about how small I am in this house, this yard,
this canyon, this galloping country and clouded horizon,

and how the people who came before us
are in their domes of earth, at peace now, so slowly turning to stone.

We're like embers that bloom from the fire into the night.
After that hour of our imagined disaster, the horses learned to wait

near the mesquite, though it changes seasons soon.
Even while you think you can't go on, the day carries you.

Limit

Our neighbors are hunting the doves
that have been safely sitting
on our fences and electric lines for months,
so tame we could nearly touch them.

Now they vanish when they see us pass the windows
and fly off in bursts when we open the doors.

On our walk, we come across one that has been injured,
a gray and brown ruffle of warmth that lies stunned.

From its side, it watches us with one round eye.
Then it flutters until it rights itself.
Well enough to stay ahead of our concern,
it is just hurt enough to starve.

The season will begin and end the same way.
The guns sound near us all morning,
then the rush of wings like souls releasing.

The hunters will shoot until they get to fifteen.

Our dogs will bark their fool heads off at the noise,
though it means nothing to them;
they keep trusting us.

Shriven

The worst part is that there is still some hope.
That there keeps being hope, no matter what happens to us.

Even though my stomach has hurt since the second grade
and I worry, one day, I won't be able to make it to work anymore.

Even though when you were a child, you couldn't say your *R*s right.
We confess our wildest disappointments to each other,

no matter how small. The ways our families' politics let us down.
The way you teach fourth grade instead of college,

though the debt we pay promised us something else.
The last rejection I got from Copper Canyon Press.

The way the plumber installed our dryer vent
(it's too long, and the angle far too steep).

The way our border collie barks day and night at nothing,
no matter how we yell at or cajole her.

And if there is room enough for her to slip past
the person who opens the gate to feed her, she will.

The last time she got by us, she did it at night,
escaped into the blackness by the road

where we could hear her rushing like a wild boar through the sage,
then catch on the bottom strand of barbed wire with a yelp

that said she didn't have the time to worry
about either her hurt or our embarrassment.

We stood in the road and could soon find no trace of her.
The darkness settled over us like a dove,

but all of the houses on the street had one bulb shining.
A quarter of a mile away, she appeared without warning

under the neighbor's porch light,
as if she had always been waiting at the wrong door.

When we called the name that should have drawn her back,
she looked our way, tongue hanging, then disappeared.

I went to get the car, but by the time I had pulled out of the driveway
you were approaching in its headlights, bent low over the dog,

the dog pulling and panting, jerking you toward home.
I rolled down the window and offered you the leash,

but you called, *It's all right— I've got her collar—*
as if we weren't talking about two different things.

That damned dog. That damned dog.

She won't stop barking at nothing.

And all this time, though there's no place left for any of us,
we keep living here. We keep confessing to one another.

Every time we are saved, we pretend it's forever.

Bate

Just to test the weight
of something that wild.
To hold a hawk's hollow-built body
in these swollen hands
though the sickness settles in the knuckles
and they tremble,
and though no one knows it yet.

You can't buy one,
though you can own it.
It is as free as a stone on a hill.
As free as flowers on the shoulder of a highway.
If you are to apprentice,
just unpin your bird from a cloud

and start to starve it.
After days of need,
you'll hold raw meat in your palm
while it watches from darkness.
You'll sing to it with lullabies of longing,
and it will start to sing them back to you.

The falconer you've questioned advises care.
Not tame enough, it won't hunt for you;
it will disappear forever into the trees.
Too tame, it won't hunt for you;
there won't be enough of a reason.

Going about your day, you think about it.
How you know where to begin now,
but still can't get there.
You take the medicine that manages the pain.
You keep your food down.
You run your hands under hot water
and flex the fingers, one by one.

You understand then.

What you must practice
is not how to be obeyed.

It is how to make something eat
even though its house is its hunger.

To the women who told me I'd never know what love meant
unless I had children

It's spring, and the coats of the horses are loosening again.
They are rubbing on the fence posts and the mesquite branches,

leaving gray and brown tufts of their winter weight.
Sparrows carry twine and horsehair to their untried nests.

Soon the sunflowers will come back, and the horses
will scratch against the stalks while they are grazing,

then come in for the night, bodies streaked with sap,
and stand in the fragrant dark, listening to coyotes yip and whine.

In the summer, hatchlings will fall around the horses from the rafters
and struggle blindly at first, eyes sealed and mouths hollow triangles,

though they are found in the evening on their backs with sunken bellies,
feet curled, skin the color of the pages of an old manuscript.

Gentle hands will gather them into an empty oat bag;
they will be coated in dust so soft it floats like a mist at the horses' fetlocks.

Horses know enough about the different kinds of loss
to ignore the pale bodies that spring brings to the barn floor.

They don't shy at the cry a rabbit makes when it is killed;
the sparrows' cries are also no concern.

When one childless person leaves another, people say *At least
it was only the two of you.* Fear could never be far enough

away from here, not the riots in the stoic cities, or the buildings that burn,
or the water poisoned, or the children who were left where they fell

for a while when the shooting stopped and events were sorted out.
Other women tell me there will never be a good time, and they are right.

Tonight, the air carries the promise of fine weather,
and the barn is filled with the earthiness of the horses, their breath,

the sound of their tails flicking, like silk rubbing against silk.
The nests from the year before are being replaced.

The sparrows from last year, the ones who made it,
add their songs to the cacophony of voices.
Each one will sing whatever song it knows.

Those that fall will be removed with tenderness.
Tell me again what love is.

Neurology

I don't look sick.
I am in the grocery store with a list.
Nothing on the shelves seems to match the words.
Have I forgotten how to read again? I wonder,
but no, the words are there; I have only
forgotten their meanings.
The person behind me clears his throat;
I am blocking the organic produce.
This is when I decide to put garlic into my cart.
Garlic makes it seem like I mean to be there.
I don't even want to think about
how far away home could be.
Someone in a green apron asks,
Can I help you find something?
I've been waiting so long
to hear it. Yes. No. I don't know.
I can't say *I am already starting to leave my body,*
so I wait too long, and say, *No, thank you.*
I am blocking the organic produce.
There is no good in trying to look too far ahead,
but maybe, when the brain unswells,
I can come back with my list and buy the right menu.
At least garlic is always useful, and it keeps.
Someday, some day a long time from now,
will I only pretend to remember us?

Wedlock

This is a poem for my mother-in-law,
who doesn't write poetry and only reads mine.

Who asks why I don't write about happiness or love
or the good things that happen to us,
but only the things that are sad or full of fear,

the things I once held that have drifted away from me
on quiet waves of darkness, and wait now beside the wake
my past has left, eyes shining and mysterious with green reflection,

and the way ahead teeming and writhing too
with things that wait to become ghosts.

I can't tell her any reason she'll accept, like
beauty doesn't need translation.

I wonder what she would think if she saw me at work,
papers scattered in an empty room, the struggle to lay down
what I know, to shake the mess of it free and stand over it,

to bend it like poor jewelry to a shape that can be worn,
though the metal is thin and it doesn't maintain the form I wanted.

And how trying to speak overcomes me, so that being in the poem
even a bad one, is like being left in a strange town
with unfamiliar streets, but I still have to find the way to places.

How the lines arrive one by one, sometimes wrestled there
in whatever order they can be made to stay still,
somehow never all the way right, never fully what I wanted.

Surely that is no way to converse about love.
Especially because the last line, another ending,
is often the most willing one, appearing even

as I stand, coffee steaming against the window,
and watch the sparrows that scratch in the dead grass
with their heads tilted, pleased by anything that isn't nothing.

I feel especially then the cold from the crack in the sill
that breathes against my knuckles, my palm against the hot cup,
and the form of the man who quietly joins me to look out
from our dual glassed reflection—

when, though his mother has never read a love poem,
and believes I do not write them,
I almost have an answer she would take.

The Onion as a Vessel of Memory

I Google *Why do onions make you cry*
meaning *me*, why *me*, but Google knows how
to parse pronouns and comes up with the answer
I'm looking for despite my lack of specificity,

that there is a vaporous compound which turns to acid
when mixed with water,
and *your eye* (mine) is the nearest source of it.

If I scroll down, strangers provide advice that I trust:
Boil water nearby to draw the vapor.
Cut the onion under a running tap.
Wear goggles. Turn on a fan.

I try all of them. I try more than all of them.
Still, I am all water and salt as I cut,
the onion a papered yellow moon that pulls,
and I can't resist it.
It seems we are inextricably tied.

My husband has learned not to be concerned
when I cry quietly over the cutting board,
feeling where to press the knife

to miss the fingers that I can't see well enough to avoid.
I remember my mother, mascara bruising her eyes

as she cut purple onions into thick quarters for a stew
and turned to speak to me

of my homework and scrapes,
all of the small childhood slights,
in a voice that sounded for all the world

as if, just that day, her heart had been broken.
As if she, too, knew how to pretend
she didn't see her mother's grief.

New Hay

I have shut the horses off their feeder again,
and they look at it through the fence with eyes that have no omega.

I can feel their yearning toward it like threads in the air.
The little hay that was left lies churned and beaten into dust,
not worth saving, and the horses have begun to feel their hunger.
Today, they have been leaning a little harder
outside of the pasture for the winter grass that's left,
rubbing off their manes in patches on the wire fence,
stretching it, making the posts lean out.

So it's time, we say, and we chase them through the gate
(not really chase, because they walk out as calmly as nuns).
They know what's happening, and they aren't afraid
that one day I won't let them back in to plenty. I have never

tested their faith. We back the truck into their pen
and push the new round bale out.
We lift the feeder, a heavy blue ring, and drop it into place.

Before I let them back in, I reach through the gate
and rub my gloved hands down their faces;
they breathe into my leather palms.

When I open the gate, they will gather at the opening
and stand still for a brief few moments,
content to study their salvation before entering it.

Then one will walk forward, and the rest will follow
forgetting, as they step through, that time of emptiness
that was the beginning of a time that might have starved them.

How, too, every mouthful brings them closer
to not having enough, when they must wait
as if outside the ending of a poem, where there is some truth
they keep reaching for and almost have.

What Happens Then

My retired mother cleans my house while I am at work
because I have become too sick to do it.
The faucets that I used to scrub with old toothbrushes,
she shines with her palms. She uses pumice stone
on the lines left by hard water. Now she runs a mop
over the dark floor in my kitchen,
watches water gleam and then dry in afterthoughts.
I suspect she gives treats to my cats, though I have asked her not to.
I know because they beg for more on days she has been there.
How comfortably they must spread around her,
eyes like narrow jewels. That is a room without any fear in it.
This morning, when I left the supplies out,
the stainless-steel spray and lemon furniture polish,
I left a note for her. I turned on the alarm. I got into my car
and backed out of the garage. In the road,
a rabbit was kicking though it must have died
a moment before when one of my neighbors hit it.
By the time I saw it, it was only holding onto its ghost.
I stopped on the shoulder then and wanted to turn back,
but I didn't. I almost never do.
Before the day's end, when I return,
something—hawk, coyote, dog— will have taken it off.
The day will already be done and undone.
I can really only guess what goes on while I am gone.
How strange that my home lives even when I am away from it.

That when I open the door some days it is to come into a place love has already been.

Autocorrect

Every time my phone changes "love" to "live,"
I wonder if it happens because my habits
have taught it what it should expect.

No one else I talk to seems to have the same problem.
Their personal devices change "talent" to "torture"
 or "kiss" to "kill" or "divorce" to "Disney"
in ways that can't be predicted.

Mine must have learned that life is more likely than love.
Having gone everywhere with me, it sees
that I have spent most of my time getting by,
buying groceries, paying bills, working
under the cold flicker of florescent lights
where my computer screen shows the small world
bending toward it, me in the middle,
and how I linger over any email, no matter how brief,
that doesn't try to sell me something.

In the meantime, I accidentally tell people
that I would live to meet for lunch
some other time, that I lived some new movie,
that I used to live the sound of instruments tuning,
and how I live the smell of pine trees.

It never works the other way;
I never lament the high cost of loving lately,

ask what someone does for a loving,
or say I'm going to see some musician play love.

I think of what I don't say that it might change:
how I try to love as well as I can,
how so often I have loved in fear.

Maybe it just knows more about it than I do,
that all those times we talked and laughed
together, what I really meant to say was
that I lived you, I lived you, I lived you.

The Fine Print of Our Vows

If I cry out, will you arrive to kill the spider
that has just been stalking me from the wall

with its green-sequined eyes?
Or (better yet), will you tell me that you

are going to put it outside into the garden,
where it will be happy wrapping its thread

around the nodding heads of flowers
for the rest of its life, until it eats its mate

or is eaten by its mate?
It's just that I'm tiring out a little.

Sometimes I get writer's block and just sit and stare.
Sometimes I forget to pay bills on time.

My body slowly thickens and my heart
flips like a bird under my ribs.

You tell me I'm still as good as I used to be,
and I try to think of that. I do.

You understand that I don't need the pressure of spiders,
the responsibility of their lives and deaths,

how my skin starts to tingle all over
with imaginary legs when I see one.

Maybe you won't take it to the garden,
maybe you never do, but if you care about me,

make me believe it.
That it is not in the trash can, crumbled with tissue,

banana peels, empty cans of vegetarian chili.
Instead, it has gone into the cool morning,

writing its message in a web shining with dew
and spinning flies into bright cocoons.

Tell me again how I still make you laugh.
Tell me again that the first time I noticed

that quiet danger that watches with its many eyes
will be the only time.

Why the Birds Return

How like a body, the bird's nest,
twist of twig re-raveled
and sewn up with what was near:
hay string, tinsel, loose fur from the spotted rabbit,
the bright ribbon from an opened gift,
set in rafters or the crook of a crooked tree
and woven into weight-holder, rain-bearer.
And how its loves fly in and out of it,
anchored to their home.
When the wind comes, or the rat tears it
to get the warm speckled eggs into its brown fingers,
the loves rebuild it into itself.
From miles away, they will keep returning to it.
It is almost never missing. It is a basin of down.
It will live as long as its loves do,
no matter how fragile, through its careful walls,
that center of song it is built around.

Daylight Saving

Today, we are the first ones awake.
If we hadn't set our alarms to maintain our routines,
we would still be in bed, wondering if the other dreamed.
The coffee maker, microwave, and oven
blink yesterday's time, as unabashedly incorrect as children.
Seven o'clock is dark again, not like it used to be,
so the sun doesn't streak across the kitchen,
doesn't shine from behind the shade
until I can't stand it anymore and have to let it all in.
It's too early now for the birds to sing.
The dogs blink at us sleepily when we let them into the yard;
confused, but willing to accept our instruction,
they stretch and yawn and reschedule their affairs.
We could do anything we wanted to them and they would accept it,
but we are not cruel. We only do even this because we have to.
Later, the antelope, who haven't learned
the shift of our traffic routines, will gawk in the road.
They will stand still, bewildered as we bear down on them and edge by.
Tomorrow, wiser, they will forage on the crest of the hill, out of reach.
The news will come on at the same time it always has,
and it will be the same news.
But the horses, we must teach to have an earlier hunger.
Later, we'll lie in bed, listening to each other breathe,
but understanding there is nothing to be said.
It's okay, this adjustment, this one more year.
Spring never lasts long enough.

This single hour of light, this one we keep,
is one we think we can redeem.

Bounding Flight

Watch birds long enough, and you'll notice
how the small ones rest while they are flying,
how they flap furiously for a long minute
and for breathtaking fractions of a second
stop, wings pressed against bodies
while they fall through emptiness.

When I think of what beauty I have seen,
it is the brown sparrow, briefly falling, I think of first.

Then, the pale breath of horses on a dark, cold night
when the stars are sharp and spinning
and every sound is brittle in the glasslike stillness.

The herons sitting around the edges of a playa lake,
fog rising from the water to mist the bellies
where one leg is tucked in white feathers;
how they don't know the lake will only be there
one month, maybe two.

The morning sun silhouetting the wind turbines
as the blades slowly turn, smooth and unreachable,
on the tips of shimmering metal towers.

The snake that lies across the hot road in the shadow
of the power lines, then slides into the summer grass
as if part of the shadow has become a soul.

The body of the doe beside the highway,
coat sparkling in the sun with frost;
behind her, the barbed wire fence lined with delicate ice.

How I have known someone who waited for me.

There are so many things I never told my parents,
who lost the baby that would have been my older sister
and watched me come into the world, not breathing at first.

And if she had survived, would I still have taken my place?

When I think of what I have seen.
The eyes of someone who used to love me.

The way the body convulses when life leaves it.

The impact of the plane hitting the second tower,
the people leaping from the windows
into the sky's blank unknown.

How everyone has their own kind of suffering.

All of it. It is almost too much to bear
for just one person, one life.

And then the birds again, the birds that will always be here,
how they alight together between electric poles, wing to wing.

How there are so many sometimes that the wire looks like it sways,
not as a result of its own heaviness,
but under the gathered weight of so many blessings.

Black Horse I Am Breaking

I knew going in that he could be the end of me.
He was slender as a long shadow,

growing taller in green silence, like the wild sunflowers
he sometimes liked to eat the tops off of;

I had to start looking up to see him.
He spooked at rumors. How carefully I have prepared him,

saddling him over and over with different disciplines,
and sending him around me at every gait and direction,

rubbing him with tarps and plastic grocery bags,
cavorting beside him to get him used to a person's silliness,

climbing on the fence and leaning over his back,
driving him across the prairie with a surcingle and long reins

while I walked behind, and the neighbors wondered
what I was up to. I am not a person who looks like

she could break a colt. No one would ever believe it.
Lovely lovely lovely beast, and terrible with strength.

How I am afraid of him, but still I can't get enough.
This is the only way I know how

to make each day leave its own bruise.
Today I must lead him back to the mounting block three times;

he keeps shifting away and chewing on my sleeve.
He is slow and calm. To him, this is only one of many hours.

On each side, I rise on arthritic knees over his back, lean,
and rub his opposite shoulder, and he watches

with his head turned so I can see one eye.
Finally I hold his head to his side so that he can't go forward yet,

put my foot in the stirrup, and then I am astride.
He has not yet intuited any of my worry. He shifts

under me, and we try to understand this new weight.
How I love him for this. How I want and don't want to outlive him.

But we haven't even begun to work, if we are lucky.
Circles and halts and half-halts. Rate and backing. Young horses

must even learn how to walk in a straight line.
It will take time and repetition. Consistency of handling.

Years of riding and surviving. Now the wind lifts his mane.
The light has risen to fill the sky. It's so bright here.

This is our last day and our first, the bravest one we'll know.

Epilogue

The Empress of Quail Canyon

As you walk down the path, not of gold,
but of dusky sage laid flat,
your subjects will flee before you.
The sparrows and juncos will cry their warning
and flit to each next tree ahead of your step.
The cottontail will scurry under a sumac
and turn to watch you as you pass,
flattening itself to a hollow in the ground.
The field rat will scramble before you
in his belief that you are pursuing him,
then veer aside into the tall grass
just beginning to stir from its chilly sleep.
You will see the rat watching from the stalks,
frozen in place, black eyes downcast in humility.
None of them will know that you intend them no harm.
That your gaze upon them is benevolent,
gracious. You will think of leaving
sunflower seeds on the path for them.
They know nothing of the world beyond the sandstone wall.
You are exactly as you appear to them,
representative with the heavy step on the dry stems;
not sick, not cruel, but alarming in stature.
When you pause, if you stay still long enough,
you will start to become invisible.
Notice how the rabbit's ears go up as he nibbles on the new shoots;
the blue quail begin to forage among the rocks.

The meadowlarks sing again, and sparrows chirp in the trees.
The longer you wait, the louder it will get,
until the sounds of those timid lives replace your own.
When you have had enough of this and continue on your errand,
you can make them hide, or freeze, or run.
The rabbit will once again press its heart to the earth.
The grasses will bend toward you in your passing.
The doe that leaps over the wall
would bow low if she knew how.

Notes

"Evergreen": The section of this poem that mentions Brussels refers to the aftermath of the March 2016 bombing of the Brussels Airport.

"The Capacity for Malignancy is Ancient": The title for this poem is taken verbatim from a statement in a CNN.com article dated July 29, 2016, entitled "Scientists Find Cancer in Million-Year-Old Fossil."

"Pathologies": "Wolf teeth… knees": These horses are immature animals. Horses grow small wolf teeth that are often removed by an equine dentist before a bit is placed in the horse's mouth for the first time. The cartilage growth plate around a horse's knee doesn't harden, or "close," until the horse is around two and a half years old. Working a horse too hard before its knees are closed could jeopardize its soundness.

"The Descent of the Germanwings": This poem was written in response to the March 2015 crash of Germanwings Flight 9525, which was deliberately caused by the plane's co-pilot.

"Googling *Borrelia burgdorferi*": *Borrelia burgdorferi* is the scientific name for the spirochete that causes Lyme borreliosis. According to the CDC, around thirty thousand cases are diagnosed every year. However, testing is faulty, diagnosis is difficult, and the CDC notes that the actual number of annual new cases may be as high as three hundred thousand.

"Staked Plains": This phrase is the translation of *Llano Estacado*, the name of the large mesa that forms most of the Texas Panhandle.

"Bate": The falconry insight in this poem is partly courtesy of talented falconer-poet Gary Worth Moody.

Thank You

My deepest gratitude goes out to the people who made this book possible, especially: Daniel Miller, who is truly and wonderfully my life partner; my parents Robert and Sherry Hammons who, along with offering other needed support, paid for medical treatment when I could not; Dallas and Todd Bell and Emily Hinds at Burrowing Owl Books, who are such wonderful people they renew my faith in the future every time I see them; my very supportive colleagues and friends at West Texas A&M University, including but not limited to Eric Meljac, Pat Tyrer, and Andy Reynolds; my good poet friends and advisors Jeff Hardin and Richard Krawiec, who never hesitate to help me when I ask them for writerly assistance; Erin Elizabeth Smith, Jeremy Michael Reed, and the team at Sundress Publications, who brought this book into the world so beautifully; Julie Greene, who advocated for me when I couldn't advocate for myself; Wade and Sonja Gross, who are always there when I need them (and love *Star Trek* as much as I do); KD, who listened to me, diagnosed my illness, began treatment, and saved my life; and Ileana and Liberty Jennings, who spread light wherever they go.

About the Author

Chera Hammons holds an MFA from Goddard College and serves as the Writer-in-Residence at West Texas A&M University. Her work has appeared in numerous literary journals and anthologies. She is the author of the novel *Monarchs of the Northeast Kingdom* and four books of poetry, including *The Traveler's Guide to Bomb City*, which received the 2017 PEN Southwest Book Award. She lives in Amarillo, TX, with her husband, three cats, three chickens, a dog, a rabbit, six horses, and a donkey.

Other Sundress Titles

JAW
Albert Abonado
$16

Lessons in Breathing Underwater
HK Hummel
$16

Bury Me in Thunder
moira j.
$16

Dead Man's Float
Ruth Foley
$16

Gender Flytrap
Zoë Estelle Hitzel
$16

Blood Stripes
Aaron Graham
$16

Boom Box
Amorak Huey
$16

Arabilis
Leah Silvieus
$16

Afakasi | Half-Caste
Hali F. Sofala-Jones
$16

Marvels
MR Sheffield
$20

Match Cut
Letitia Trent
$16

Passing Through Humansville
Karen Craigo
$16

Divining Bones
Charlie Bondus
$16

Phantom Tongue
Steven Sanchez
$15

www.ingramcontent.com/pod-product-compliance
Lightning Source LLC
Chambersburg PA
CBHW081418090426
42738CB00017B/3412